'A masterly picture of despair and optimism whose vivid alterations seem to characterize so much of Latin American life. He dazzles us with powerful effect' *New Statesman*

'Márquez writes in this lyrical, magical language that no-one else can do' Salman Rushdie

'Of all the living authors known to me, only one is undoubtedly touched by genius: Gabriel García Márquez' *Sunday Telegraph*

'The most important writer of fiction in any language' Bill Clinton

'An imaginative writer of genius, the topmost pinnacle of an entire generation of Latin American novelists of cathedral-like proportions' *Guardian*

'One of this century's most evocative writers' Anne Tyler

'Márquez is a retailer of wonders' *Sunday Times*

'Sentence for sentence, there is hardly another writer in the world so generous with incidental pleasures' *Independent*

GABRIEL GARCÍA MÁRQUEZ

NO ONE WRITES TO
THE COLONEL

TRANSLATED BY J. S. BERNSTEIN

PENGUIN BOOKS

PENGUIN BOOKS

Published by the Penguin Group
Penguin Books Ltd, 80 Strand, London WC2R ORL, England
Penguin Group (USA) Inc., 375 Hudson Street, New York, New York 10014, USA
Penguin Group (Canada), 90 Eglinton Avenue East, Suite 700, Toronto, Ontario, Canada M4P 2Y3
(a division of Pearson Penguin Canada Inc.)
Penguin Ireland, 25 St Stephen's Green, Dublin 2, Ireland (a division of Penguin Books Ltd)
Penguin Group (Australia), 250 Camberwell Road, Camberwell, Victoria 3124, Australia
(a division of Pearson Australia Group Pty Ltd)
Penguin Books India Pvt Ltd, 11 Community Centre, Panchsheel Park, New Delhi – 110 017, India
Penguin Group (NZ), 67 Apollo Drive, Rosedale, North Shore 0632, New Zealand
(a division of Pearson New Zealand Ltd)
Penguin Books (South Africa) (Pty) Ltd, 24 Sturdee Avenue,
Rosebank, Johannesburg 2196, South Africa

Penguin Books Ltd, Registered Offices: 80 Strand, London WC2R ORL, England

www.penguin.com

First published in Spanish as *El Coronel No Tiene Quien Le Escribe*
This translation first published in the United States of America by
Harper & Row, Publishers, Inc., 1968 and in Great Britain by Jonathan Cape 1971
First published in Penguin Books 1974
This edition published 2008

4

English translation copyright © Harper & Row, Publishers, Inc., 1968
All rights reserved

The moral right of the author has been asserted

Printed in England by Clays Ltd, St Ives plc

ISBN: 978-0-141-03253-5

www.greenpenguin.co.uk

The colonel took the top off the coffee can and saw that there was only one little spoonful left. He removed the pot from the fire, poured half the water onto the earthen floor, and scraped the inside of the can with a knife until the last scrapings of the ground coffee, mixed with bits of rust, fell into the pot.

While he was waiting for it to boil, sitting next to the stone fireplace with an attitude of confident and innocent expectation, the colonel experienced the feeling that fungus and poisonous lilies were taking root in his gut. It was October. A difficult morning to get through, even for a man like himself, who had survived so many mornings like this one. For nearly sixty years – since the end of the last civil war – the colonel had done nothing else but wait. October was one of the few things which arrived.

His wife raised the mosquito netting when she saw him come into the bedroom with the coffee. The night before she had suffered an asthma attack, and now she was in a drowsy state. But she sat up to take the cup.

'And you?' she said.

'I've had mine,' the colonel lied. 'There was still a big spoonful left.'

The bells began ringing at that moment. The colonel had forgotten the funeral. While his wife was drinking her coffee, he unhooked the hammock at one end, and rolled it up on the other, behind the door. The woman thought about the dead man.

'He was born in 1922,' she said. 'Exactly a month after our son. April 7th.'

She continued sipping her coffee in the pauses of her gravelly breathing. She was scarcely more than a bit of white on an arched, rigid spine. Her disturbed breathing made her put her questions as assertions. When she finished her coffee, she was still thinking about the dead man.

'It must be horrible to be buried in October,' she said. But her husband paid no attention. He opened the window. October had moved in on the patio. Contemplating the vegetation, which was bursting out in intense greens, and the tiny mounds the worms made in the mud, the colonel felt the sinister month again in his intestines.

'I'm wet through to the bones,' he said.

'It's winter,' the woman replied. 'Since it began raining I've been telling you to sleep with your socks on.'

'I've been sleeping with them for a week.'

It rained gently but ceaselessly. The colonel would have preferred to wrap himself in a wool blanket and get back into the hammock. But the insistence of the cracked bells reminded him about the funeral. 'It's October,' he whispered, and walked toward the center of the room. Only then did he remember the rooster tied to the leg of the bed. It was a fighting cock.

After taking the cup into the kitchen, he wound the pendulum clock in its carved wooden case in the living room. Unlike the bedroom, which was too narrow for an asthmatic's breathing, the living room was large,

2

with four sturdy rockers around a little table with a cover and a plaster cat. On the wall opposite the clock, there was a picture of a woman dressed in tulle, surrounded by cupids in a boat laden with roses.

It was seven-twenty when he finished winding the clock. Then he took the rooster into the kitchen, tied it to a leg of the stove, changed the water in the can, and put a handful of corn next to it. A group of children came in through a hole in the fence. They sat around the rooster, to watch it in silence.

'Stop looking at that animal,' said the colonel. 'Roosters wear out if you look at them so much.'

The children didn't move. One of them began playing the chords of a popular song on his harmonica. 'Don't play that today,' the colonel told him. 'There's been a death in town.' The child put the instrument in his pants pocket, and the colonel went into the bedroom to dress for the funeral.

Because of his wife's asthma, his white suit was not pressed. So he had to wear the old black suit which since his marriage he used only on special occasions. It took some effort to find it in the bottom of the trunk, wrapped in newspapers and protected against moths with little balls of naphthalene. Stretched out in bed, the woman was still thinking about the dead man.

'He must have met Agustín already,' she said. 'Maybe he won't tell him about the situation we've been left in since his death.'

'At this moment they're probably talking roosters,' said the colonel.

He found an enormous old umbrella in the trunk. His wife had won it in a raffle held to collect funds for the colonel's party. That same night they had attended an outdoor show which was not interrupted despite the rain. The colonel, his wife, and their son, Agustín – who was then eight – watched the show until the end, seated under the umbrella. Now Agustín was dead, and the bright satin material had been eaten away by the moths.

'Look what's left of our circus clown's umbrella,' said the colonel with one of his old phrases. Above his head a mysterious system of little metal rods opened. 'The only thing it's good for now is to count the stars.'

He smiled. But the woman didn't take the trouble to look at the umbrella. 'Everything's that way,' she whispered. 'We're rotting alive.' And she closed her eyes so she could concentrate on the dead man.

After shaving himself by touch – since he'd lacked a mirror for a long time – the colonel dressed silently. His trousers, almost as tight on his legs as long underwear, closed at the ankles with slip-knotted drawstrings, were held up at the waist by two straps of the same material which passed through two gilt buckles sewn on at kidney height. He didn't use a belt. His shirt, the color of old Manila paper, and as stiff, fastened with a copper stud which served at the same time to hold the detachable collar. But the detachable collar was torn, so the colonel gave up on the idea of a tie.

He did each thing as if it were a transcendent act. The bones in his hands were covered by taut, translucent skin, with light spots like the skin on his neck. Before he put on his patent-leather shoes, he scraped the dried mud from the stitching. His wife saw him at that moment, dressed as he was on their wedding day. Only then did she notice how much her husband had aged.

4

'You look as if you're dressed for some special event,' she said.

'This burial is a special event,' the colonel said. 'It's the first death from natural causes which we've had in many years.'

The weather cleared up after nine. The colonel was getting ready to go out when his wife seized him by the sleeve of his coat.

'Comb your hair,' she said.

He tried to subdue his steel-colored, bristly hair with a bone comb. But it was a useless attempt.

'I must look like a parrot,' he said.

The woman examined him. She thought he didn't. The colonel didn't look like a parrot. He was a dry man, with solid bones articulated as if with nuts and bolts. Because of the vitality in his eyes, it didn't seem as if he were preserved in formalin.

'You're fine that way,' she admitted, and added, when her husband was leaving the room: 'Ask the doctor if we poured boiling water on him in this house.'

They lived at the edge of town, in a house with a palm-thatched roof and walls whose whitewash was flaking off. The humidity kept up but the rain had stopped. The colonel went down toward the plaza along an alley with houses crowded in on each other. As he came out into the main street, he shivered. As far as the eye could see, the town was carpeted with flowers. Seated in their doorways, the women in black were waiting for the funeral.

In the plaza it began to drizzle again. The proprietor of the pool hall saw the colonel from the door of his place and shouted to him with open arms: 'Colonel, wait, and I'll lend you an umbrella!'

The colonel replied without turning around. 'Thank you. I'm all right this way.'

The funeral procession hadn't come out of church yet. The men – dressed in white with black ties – were talking in the low doorway under their umbrellas. One of them saw the colonel jumping between the puddles in the plaza.

'Get under here, friend!' he shouted.

He made room under the umbrella.

'Thanks, friend,' said the colonel.

But he didn't accept the invitation. He entered the house directly to give his condolences to the mother of the dead man. The first thing he perceived was the odor of many different flowers. Then the heat rose. The colonel tried to make his way through the crowd which was jammed into the bedroom. But someone put a hand on his back, pushed him toward the back of the room through a gallery of perplexed faces to the spot where – deep and wide open – the nostrils of the dead man were found.

There was the dead man's mother, shooing the flies away from the coffin with a plaited palm fan. Other women, dressed in black, contemplated the body with the same expression with which one watches the current of a river. All at once a voice started up at the back of the room. The colonel put one woman aside, faced the profile of the dead man's mother, and put a hand on her shoulder.

'I'm so sorry,' he said.

She didn't turn her head. She opened her mouth and

let out a howl. The colonel started. He felt himself being pushed against the corpse by a shapeless crowd which broke out in a quavering outcry. He looked for a firm support for his hands but couldn't find the wall. There were other bodies in its place. Someone said in his ear, slowly, with a very gentle voice, 'Careful, colonel.' He spun his head around and was face to face with the dead man. But he didn't recognize him because he was stiff and dynamic and seemed as disconcerted as he, wrapped in white cloths and with his trumpet in his hands. When the colonel raised his head over the shouts, in search of air, he saw the closed box bouncing toward the door down a slope of flowers which disintegrated against the walls. He perspired. His joints ached. A moment later he knew he was in the street because the drizzle hurt his eyelids, and someone seized him by the arm and said:

'Hurry up, friend, I was waiting for you.'

It was Sabas, the godfather of his dead son, the only leader of his party who had escaped political persecution and had continued to live in town. 'Thanks, friend,' said the colonel, and walked in silence under the umbrella. The band struck up the funeral march. The colonel noticed the lack of a trumpet, and for the first time was certain that the dead man was dead.

'Poor man,' he murmured.

Sabas cleared his throat. He held the umbrella in his left hand, the handle almost at the level of his head, since he was shorter than the colonel. They began to talk when the cortege left the plaza. Sabas turned toward the colonel then, his face disconsolate, and said: 'Friend, what's new with the rooster?'

'He's still there,' the colonel replied.

At that moment a shout was heard: 'Where are they going with that dead man?'

The colonel raised his eyes. He saw the mayor on the balcony of the barracks in an expansive pose. He was dressed in his flannel underwear; his unshaven cheek was swollen. The musicians stopped the march. A moment later the colonel recognized Father Ángel's voice shouting at the mayor. He made out their dialogue through the drumming of the rain on the umbrella.

'Well?' asked Sabas.

'Well nothing,' the colonel replied. 'The burial may not pass in front of the police barracks.'

'I had forgotten,' exclaimed Sabas. 'I always forget that we are under martial law.'

'But this isn't a rebellion,' the colonel said. 'It's a poor dead musician.'

The cortege changed direction. In the poor neighborhoods the women watched it pass, biting their nails in silence. But then they came out into the middle of the street and sent up shouts of praise, gratitude, and farewell, as if they believed the dead man was listening to them inside the coffin. The colonel felt ill at the cemetery. When Sabas pushed him toward the wall to make way for the men who were carrying the dead man, he turned his smiling face toward him, but met a rigid countenance.

'What's the matter, friend?' Sabas asked.

The colonel sighed. 'It's October.'

They returned by the same street. It had cleared. The sky was deep, intensely blue. It won't rain any more, thought the colonel, and he felt better, but he was still dejected. Sabas interrupted his thoughts.

'Have a doctor examine you.'

'I'm not sick,' the colonel said. 'The trouble is that in October I feel as if I had animals in my gut.'

Sabas went 'Ah.' He said goodbye at the door to his house, a new building, two stories high, with wrought-iron window gratings. The colonel headed for his home, anxious to take off his dress suit. He went out again a moment later to the store on the corner to buy a can of coffee and half a pound of corn for the rooster.

The colonel attended to the rooster in spite of the fact that on Thursday he would have preferred to stay in his hammock. It didn't clear for several days. During the course of the week, the flora in his belly blossomed. He spent several sleepless nights, tormented by the whistling of the asthmatic woman's lungs. But October granted a truce on Friday afternoon. Agustín's companions – workers from the tailor shop, as he had been, and cockfight fanatics – took advantage of the occasion to examine the rooster. He was in good shape.

The colonel returned to the bedroom when he was left alone in the house with his wife. She had recovered.

'What do they say?' she asked.

'Very enthusiastic,' the colonel informed her. 'Everyone is saving their money to bet on the rooster.'

'I don't know what they see in such an ugly rooster,' the woman said. 'He looks like a freak to me; his head is too tiny for his feet.'

'They say he's the best in the district,' the colonel answered. 'He's worth about fifty pesos.'

He was sure that this argument justified his determination to keep the rooster, a legacy from their son who was shot down nine months before at the cockfights for distributing clandestine literature. 'An expensive illusion,' she said. 'When the corn is gone we'll have to feed him on our own livers.' The colonel took a good long time to think, while he was looking for his white ducks in the closet.

'It's just for a few months,' he said. 'We already know that there will be fights in January. Then we can sell him for more.'

The pants needed pressing. The woman stretched them out over the stove with two irons heated over the coals.

'What's your hurry to go out?' she asked.

'The mail.'

'I had forgotten that today is Friday,' she commented, returning to the bedroom. The colonel was dressed but pants-less. She observed his shoes.

'Those shoes are ready to throw out,' she said. 'Keep wearing your patent-leather ones.'

The colonel felt desolate.

'They look like the shoes of an orphan,' he protested. 'Every time I put them on I feel like a fugitive from an asylum.'

'We are the orphans of our son,' the woman said.

This time, too, she persuaded him. The colonel walked toward the harbor before the whistles of the launches blew. Patent-leather shoes, beltless white ducks, and the shirt without the detachable collar, closed at the neck with the copper stud. He observed the docking of the launches from the shop of Moses the Syrian. The travelers got off, stiff from eight hours of immobility. The same ones as always: traveling sales-men, and people from the town who had left the preceding week and were returning as usual.

The last one was the mail launch. The colonel saw it dock with an anguished uneasiness. On the roof, tied to the boat's smokestacks and protected by an oilcloth, he spied the mailbag. Fifteen years of waiting had sharpened his intuition. The rooster had sharpened his anxiety. From the moment the postmaster went on board the launch, untied the bag, and hoisted it up on his shoulder, the colonel kept him in sight.

He followed him through the street parallel to the harbor, a labyrinth of stores and booths with colored merchandise on display. Every time he did it, the colonel experienced an anxiety very different from, but just as oppressive as, fright. The doctor was waiting for the newspapers in the post office.

'My wife wants me to ask you if we threw boiling water on you at our house,' the colonel said.

He was a young physician with his skull covered by sleek black hair. There was something unbelievable in the perfection of his dentition. He asked after the health of the asthmatic. The colonel supplied a detailed report without taking his eyes off the postmaster, who was distributing the letters into cubbyholes. His indolent way of moving exasperated the colonel.

The doctor received his mail with the packet of news-papers. He put the pamphlets of medical advertising to one side. Then he scanned his personal letters. Mean-while the postmaster was handing out mail to those who were present. The colonel watched the compart-ment which corresponded to his letter in the alphabet.

An air-mail letter with blue borders increased his nervous tension.

The doctor broke the seal on the newspapers. He read the lead items while the colonel – his eyes fixed on the little box – waited for the postmaster to stop in front of it. But he didn't. The doctor interrupted his reading of the newspapers. He looked at the colonel. Then he looked at the postmaster seated in front of the telegraph key, and then again at the colonel.

'We're leaving,' he said.

The postmaster didn't raise his head.

'Nothing for the colonel,' he said.

The colonel felt ashamed.

'I wasn't expecting anything,' he lied. He turned to the doctor with an entirely childish look. 'No one writes to me.'

They went back in silence. The doctor was concentrating on the newspapers. The colonel with his habitual way of walking which resembled that of a man retracing his steps to look for a lost coin. It was a bright afternoon. The almond trees in the plaza were shedding their last rotted leaves. It had begun to grow dark when they arrived at the door of the doctor's office.

'What's in the news?' the colonel asked.

The doctor gave him a few newspapers.

'No one knows,' he said. 'It's hard to read between the lines which the censor lets them print.'

The colonel read the main headlines. International news. At the top, across four columns, a report on the Suez Canal. The front page was almost completely covered by paid funeral announcements.

'There's no hope of elections,' the colonel said.

'Don't be naïve, colonel,' said the doctor. 'We're too old now to be waiting for the Messiah.'

The colonel tried to give the newspapers back, but the doctor refused them.

'Take them home with you,' he said. 'You can read them tonight and return them tomorrow.'

A little after seven the bells in the tower rang out the censor's movie classifications. Father Ángel used this means to announce the moral classification of the film in accordance with the ratings he received every month by mail. The colonel's wife counted twelve bells.

'Unfit for everyone,' she said. 'It's been about a year now that the movies are bad for everyone.'

She lowered the mosquito netting and murmured, 'The world is corrupt.' But the colonel made no comment. Before lying down, he tied the rooster to the leg of the bed. He locked the house and sprayed some insecticide in the bedroom. Then he put the lamp on the floor, hung his hammock up, and lay down to read the newspapers.

He read them in chronological order, from the first page to the last, including the advertisements. At eleven the trumpet blew curfew. The colonel finished his reading a half-hour later, opened the patio door on the impenetrable night, and urinated, besieged by mosquitoes, against the wall studs. His wife was awake when he returned to the bedroom.

'Nothing about the veterans?' she asked.

'Nothing,' said the colonel. He put out the lamp before he got into the hammock. 'In the beginning at least they published the list of the new pensioners. But it's been about five years since they've said anything.'

It rained after midnight. The colonel managed to get to sleep but woke up a moment later, alarmed by his intestines. He discovered a leak in some part of the roof. Wrapped in a wool blanket up to his ears, he tried to find the leak in the darkness. A trickle of cold sweat slipped down his spine. He had a fever. He felt as if he were floating in concentric circles inside a tank of jelly. Someone spoke. The colonel answered from his revolutionist's cot.

'Who are you talking to?' asked his wife.

'The Englishman disguised as a tiger who appeared at Colonel Aureliano Buendía's camp,' the colonel answered. He turned over in his hammock, burning with his fever. 'It was the Duke of Marlborough.'

The sky was clear at dawn. At the second call for Mass, he jumped from the hammock and installed himself in a confused reality which was agitated by the crowing of the rooster. His head was still spinning in concentric circles. He was nauseous. He went out into the patio and headed for the privy through the barely audible whispers and the dark odors of winter. The inside of the little zinc-roofed wooden compartment was rarefied by the ammonia smell from the privy. When the colonel raised the lid, a triangular cloud of flies rushed out of the pit.

It was a false alarm. Squatting on the platform of unsanded boards, he felt the uneasiness of an urge frustrated. The oppressiveness was substituted by a dull ache in his digestive tract. 'There's no doubt,' he murmured. 'It's the same every October.' And again he assumed his posture of confident and innocent expectation until the fungus in his innards was pacified. Then he returned to the bedroom for the rooster.

'Last night you were delirious from fever,' his wife said.

She had begun to straighten up the room, having recovered from a week-long attack. The colonel made an effort to remember.

'It wasn't fever,' he lied. 'It was the dream about the spider webs again.'

As always happened, the woman emerged from her attack full of nervous energy. In the course of the morning she turned the house upside down. She changed the position of everything, except the clock and the picture of the young girl. She was so thin and sinewy that when she walked about in her cloth slippers and her black dress all buttoned up she seemed as if she had the power of walking through the walls. But before twelve she had regained her bulk, her human weight. In bed she was an empty space. Now, moving among the flower-pots of ferns and begonias, her presence overflowed the house. 'If Agustín's year were up, I would start singing,' she said while she stirred the pot where all the things to eat that the tropical land is capable of producing, cut into pieces, were boiling.

'If you feel like singing, sing,' said the colonel. 'It's good for your spleen.'

The doctor came after lunch. The colonel and his wife were drinking coffee in the kitchen when he pushed open the street door and shouted:

'Everybody dead?'

The colonel got up to welcome him.

'So it seems, doctor,' he said, going into the living room. 'I've always said that your clock keeps time with the buzzards.'

The woman went into the bedroom to get ready for the examination. The doctor stayed in the living room with the colonel. In spite of the heat, his immaculate linen suit gave off a smell of freshness. When the woman announced that she was ready, the doctor gave the colonel three sheets of paper in an envelope. He entered the bedroom, saying, 'That's what the newspapers didn't print yesterday.'

The colonel had assumed as much. It was a summary of the events in the country, mimeographed for clandestine circulation. Revelations about the state of armed resistance in the interior of the country. He felt defeated. Ten years of clandestine reports had not taught him that no news was more surprising than next month's news. He had finished reading when the doctor came back into the living room.

'This patient is healthier than I am,' he said. 'With asthma like that, I could live to be a hundred.'

The colonel glowered at him. He gave him back the envelope without saying a word, but the doctor refused to take it.

'Pass it on,' he said in a whisper.

The colonel put the envelope in his pants pocket. The woman came out of the bedroom, saying, 'One of these days I'll up and die, and carry you with me, off to hell, doctor.' The doctor responded silently with the stereotyped enamel of his teeth. He pulled a chair up to the little table and took several jars of free samples out of his bag. The woman went on into the kitchen.

'Wait and I'll warm up the coffee.'

'No, thank you very much,' said the doctor. He wrote

the proper dosage on a prescription pad. 'I absolutely refuse to give you the chance to poison me.'

She laughed in the kitchen. When he finished writing, the doctor read the prescription aloud, because he knew that no one could decipher his handwriting. The colonel tried to concentrate. Returning from the kitchen, the woman discovered in his face the toll of the previous night.

'This morning he had a fever,' she said, pointing at her husband. 'He spent about two hours talking nonsense about the civil war.'

The colonel started.

'It wasn't a fever,' he insisted, regaining his composure. 'Furthermore,' he said, 'the day I feel sick I'll throw myself into the garbage can on my own.'

He went into the bedroom to find the newspapers.

'Thank you for the compliment,' the doctor said.

They walked together toward the plaza. The air was dry. The tar on the streets had begun to melt from the heat. When the doctor said goodbye, the colonel asked him in a low voice, his teeth clenched: 'How much do we owe you, doctor?'

'Nothing, for now,' the doctor said, and he gave him a pat on the shoulder. 'I'll send you a fat bill when the cock wins.'

The colonel went to the tailor shop to take the clandestine letter to Agustín's companions. It was his only refuge ever since his co-partisans had been killed or exiled from town and he had been converted into a man with no other occupation than waiting for the mail every Friday.

The afternoon heat stimulated the woman's energy.

Seated among the begonias in the veranda next to a box of worn-out clothing, she was again working the eternal miracle of creating new apparel out of nothing. She made collars from sleeves, and cuffs from the backs and square patches, perfect ones, although with scraps of different colors. A cicada lodged its whistle in the patio. The sun faded. But she didn't see it go down over the begonias. She raised her head only at dusk when the colonel returned home. Then she clasped her neck with both hands, cracked her knuckles, and said:

'My head is as stiff as a board.'

'It's always been that way,' the colonel said, but then he saw his wife's body covered all over with scraps of color. 'You look like a magpie,'

'One has to be half a magpie to dress you,' she said. She held out a shirt made of three different colors of material except for the collar and cuffs, which were of the same color. 'At the carnival all you have to do is take off your jacket.'

The six-o'clock bells interrupted her. 'The Angel of the Lord announced unto Mary,' she prayed aloud, heading into the bedroom. The colonel talked to the children who had come to look at the rooster after school. Then he remembered that there was no corn for the next day, and entered the bedroom to ask his wife for money.

'I think there's only fifty cents,' she said.

She kept the money under the mattress, knotted into the corner of a handkerchief. It was the proceeds of Agustín's sewing machine. For nine months, they had spent that money penny by penny, parceling it out between their needs and the rooster's. Now there were only two twenty-cent pieces and a ten-cent piece left.

18

'Buy a pound of corn,' the woman said. 'With the change, buy tomorrow's coffee and four ounces of cheese.'

'And a golden elephant to hang in the doorway,' the colonel went on. 'The corn alone costs forty-two.'

They thought for a moment. 'The rooster is an animal, and therefore he can wait,' said the woman at first. But her husband's expression caused her to reflect. The colonel sat on the bed, his elbows on his knees, jingling the coins in his hands. 'It's not for my sake,' he said after a moment. 'If it depended on me I'd make a rooster stew this very evening. A fifty-peso indigestion would be very good.' He paused to squash a mosquito on his neck. Then his eyes followed his wife around the room.

'What bothers me is that those poor boys are saving up.'

Then she began to think. She turned completely around with the insecticide bomb. The colonel found something unreal in her attitude, as if she were invoking the spirits of the house for a consultation. At last she put the bomb on the little mantel with the prints on it, and fixed her syrup-colored eyes on the syrup-colored eyes of the colonel.

'Buy the corn,' she said. 'God knows how we'll manage.'

'This is the miracle of the multiplying loaves,' the colonel repeated every time they sat down to the table during the following week. With her astonishing capacity for darning, sewing, and mending, she seemed to have discovered the key to sustaining the household economy with no money. October prolonged its truce. The humidity was replaced by sleepiness. Comforted by the copper sun, the woman devoted three afternoons to her complicated hairdo. 'High Mass has begun,' the colonel said one afternoon when she was getting the knots out of her long blue tresses with a comb which had some teeth missing. The second afternoon, seated in the patio with a white sheet in her lap, she used a finer comb to take out the lice which had proliferated during her attack. Lastly, she washed her hair with lavender water, waited for it to dry, and rolled it up on the nape of her neck in two turns held with a barrette. The colonel waited. At night, sleepless in his hammock, he worried for many hours over the rooster's fate. But on Wednesday they weighed him, and he was in good shape.

That same afternoon, when Agustín's companions left the house counting the imaginary proceeds from the rooster's victory, the colonel also felt in good shape. His wife cut his hair. 'You've taken twenty years off me,' he said, examining his head with his hands. His wife thought her husband was right.

'When I'm well, I can bring back the dead,' she said.

But her conviction lasted for a very few hours. There was no longer anything in the house to sell, except the clock and the picture. Thursday night, at the limit of their resources, the woman showed her anxiety over the situation.

'Don't worry,' the colonel consoled her. 'The mail comes tomorrow.'

The following day he waited for the launches in front of the doctor's office.

'The airplane is a marvelous thing,' the colonel said,

his eyes resting on the mailbag. 'They say you can get to Europe in one night.'

'That's right,' the doctor said, fanning himself with an illustrated magazine. The colonel spied the postmaster among a group waiting for the docking to end so they could jump onto the launch. The postmaster jumped first. He received from the captain an envelope sealed with wax. Then he climbed up onto the roof. The mailbag was tied between two oil drums.

'But still it has its dangers,' said the colonel. He lost the postmaster from sight, but saw him again among the colored bottles on the refreshment cart. 'Humanity doesn't progress without paying a price.'

'Even at this stage it's safer than a launch,' the doctor said. 'At twenty thousand feet you fly above the weather.'

'Twenty thousand feet,' the colonel repeated, perplexed, without being able to imagine what the figure meant.

The doctor became interested. He spread out the magazine with both hands until it was absolutely still.

'There's perfect stability,' he said.

But the colonel was hanging on the actions of the postmaster. He saw him consume a frothy pink drink, holding the glass in his left hand. In his right he held the mailbag.

'Also, on the ocean there are ships at anchor in continual contact with night flights,' the doctor went on. 'With so many precautions it's safer than a launch.'

The colonel looked at him.

'Naturally,' he said. 'It must be like a carpet.'

The postmaster came straight toward them. The

colonel stepped back, impelled by an irresistible anxiety, trying to read the name written on the sealed envelope. The postmaster opened the bag. He gave the doctor his packet of newspapers. Then he tore open the envelope with the personal correspondence, checked the correctness of the receipt, and read the addressee's names off the letters. The doctor opened the newspapers.

'Still the problem with Suez,' he said, reading the main headlines. 'The West is losing ground.'

The colonel didn't read the headlines. He made an effort to control his stomach. 'Ever since there's been censorship, the newspapers talk only about Europe,' he said. 'The best thing would be for the Europeans to come over here and for us to go to Europe. That way everybody would know what's happening in his own country.'

'To the Europeans, South America is a man with a mustache, a guitar, and a gun,' the doctor said, laughing over his newspaper. 'They don't understand the problem.'

The postmaster delivered his mail. He put the rest in the bag and closed it again. The doctor got ready to read two personal letters, but before tearing open the envelopes he looked at the colonel. Then he looked at the postmaster.

'Nothing for the colonel?'

The colonel was terrified. The postmaster tossed the bag onto his shoulder, got off the platform, and replied without turning his head: 'No one writes to the colonel.'

Contrary to his habit, he didn't go directly home. He had a cup of coffee at the tailor's while Agustín's companions leafed through the newspapers. He felt cheated. He would have preferred to stay there until the next Friday to keep from having to face his wife that night with empty hands. But when the tailor shop closed, he had to face up to reality. His wife was waiting for him.

'Nothing?' she asked.

'Nothing,' the colonel answered.

The following Friday he went down to the launches again. And, as on every Friday, he returned home without the longed-for letter. 'We've waited long enough,' his wife told him that night. 'One must have the patience of an ox, as you do, to wait for a letter for fifteen years.' The colonel got into his hammock to read the newspapers.

'We have to wait our turn,' he said. 'Our number is 1823.'

'Since we've been waiting, that number has come up twice in the lottery,' his wife replied.

The colonel read, as usual, from the first page to the last, including the advertisements. But this time he didn't concentrate. During his reading, he thought about his veteran's pension. Nineteen years before, when Congress passed the law, it took him eight years to prove his claim. Then it took him six more years to get himself included on the rolls. That was the last letter the colonel had received.

He finished after curfew sounded. When he went to turn off the lamp, he realized that his wife was awake.

'Do you still have that clipping?'

The woman thought.

'Yes. It must be with the other papers.'

She got out of her mosquito netting and took a

wooden chest out of the closet, with a packet of letters arranged by date and held together by a rubber band. She located the advertisement of a law firm which promised quick action on war pensions.

'We could have spent the money in the time I've wasted trying to convince you to change lawyers,' the woman said, handing her husband the newspaper clipping. 'We're not getting anything out of their putting us away on a shelf as they do with the Indians.'

The colonel read the clipping dated two years before. He put it in the pocket of his jacket which was hanging behind the door.

'The problem is that to change lawyers you need money.'

'Not at all,' the woman said decisively. 'You write them telling them to discount whatever they want from the pension itself when they collect it. It's the only way they'll take the case.'

So Saturday afternoon the colonel went to see his lawyer. He found him stretched out lazily in a hammock. He was a monumental negro, with nothing but two canines in his upper jaw. The lawyer put his feet into a pair of wooden-soled slippers and opened the office window on a dusty pianola with papers stuffed into the compartments where the rolls used to go: clippings from the *Official Gazette*, pasted into old accounting ledgers, and a jumbled collection of accounting bulletins. The keyless pianola did double duty as a desk. The lawyer sat down in a swivel chair. The colonel expressed his uneasiness before revealing the purpose of his visit.

'I warned you that it would take more than a few days,' said the lawyer when the colonel paused. He was sweltering in the heat. He adjusted the chair backward and fanned himself with an advertising brochure.

'My agents write to me frequently, saying not to get impatient.'

'It's been that way for fifteen years,' the colonel answered. 'This is beginning to sound like the story about the capon.'

The lawyer gave a very graphic description of the administrative ins and outs. The chair was too narrow for his sagging buttocks. 'Fifteen years ago it was easier,' he said. 'Then there was the city's veterans' organization, with members of both parties.' His lungs filled with stifling air and he pronounced the sentence as if he had just invented it: 'There's strength in numbers.'

'There wasn't in this case,' the colonel said, realizing his aloneness for the first time. 'All my comrades died waiting for the mail.'

The lawyer didn't change his expression.

'The law was passed too late,' he said. 'Not everybody was as lucky as you to be a colonel at the age of twenty. Furthermore, no special allocation was included, so the government has had to make adjustments in the budget.'

Always the same story. Each time the colonel listened to him, he felt a mute resentment. 'This is not charity,' he said. 'It's not a question of doing us a favor. We broke our backs to save the Republic.' The lawyer threw up his hands.

'That's the way it is,' he said. 'Human ingratitude knows no limits.'

The colonel also knew that story. He had begun

hearing it the day after the Treaty of Neerlandia, when the government promised travel assistance and indemnities to two hundred revolutionary officers. Camped at the base of the gigantic silk-cotton tree at Neerlandia, a revolutionary battalion, made up in great measure of youths who had left school, waited for three months. Then they went back to their homes by their own means, and they kept on waiting there. Almost sixty years later, the colonel was still waiting.

Excited by these memories, he adopted a transcendental attitude. He rested his right hand on his thigh – mere bone sewed together with nerve tissue – and murmured:

'Well, I've decided to take action.'

The lawyer waited.

'Such as?'

'To change lawyers.'

A mother duck, followed by several little ducklings, entered the office. The lawyer sat up to chase them out. 'As you wish, colonel,' he said, chasing the animals. 'It will be just as you wish. If I could work miracles, I wouldn't be living in this barnyard.' He put a wooden grille across the patio door and returned to his chair.

'My son worked all his life,' said the colonel. 'My house is mortgaged. That retirement law has been a lifetime pension for lawyers.'

'Not for me,' the lawyer protested. 'Every last cent has gone for my expenses.'

The colonel suffered at the thought that he had been unjust.

'That's what I meant,' he corrected himself. He dried his forehead with the sleeve of his shirt. 'This heat is enough to rust the screws in your head.'

A moment later the lawyer was turning the office upside down looking for the power of attorney. The sun advanced toward the center of the tiny room, which was built of unsanded boards. After looking futilely everywhere, the lawyer got down on all fours, huffing and puffing, and picked up a roll of papers from under the pianola.

'Here it is.'

He gave the colonel a sheet of paper with a seal on it. 'I have to write my agents so they can cancel the copies,' he concluded. The colonel shook the dust off the paper and put it in his shirt pocket.

'Tear it up yourself,' the lawyer said.

'No,' the colonel answered. 'These are twenty years of memories.' And he waited for the lawyer to keep on looking. But the lawyer didn't. He went to the hammock to wipe off his sweat. From there he looked at the colonel through the shimmering air.

'I need the documents also,' the colonel said.

'Which ones?'

'The proof of claim.'

The lawyer threw up his hands.

'Now, that would be impossible, colonel.'

The colonel became alarmed. As Treasurer of the revolution in the district of Macondo, he had undertaken a difficult six-day journey with the funds for the civil war in two trunks roped to the back of a mule. He arrived at the camp of Neerlandia dragging the mule, which was dead from hunger, half an hour before the treaty was signed. Colonel Aureliano Buendía – quartermaster general of the revolutionary forces on the Atlantic coast – held out the receipt for the funds, and included the two trunks in his inventory of the surrender.

'Those documents have an incalculable value,' the colonel said. 'There's a receipt from Colonel Aureliano Buendía, written in his own hand.'

'I agree,' said the lawyer. 'But those documents have passed through thousands and thousands of hands, in thousands and thousands of offices, before they reached God knows which department in the War Ministry.'

'No official could fail to notice documents like those,' the colonel said.

'But the officials have changed many times in the last fifteen years,' the lawyer pointed out. 'Just think about it; there have been seven presidents, and each president changed his cabinet at least ten times, and each minister changed his staff at least a hundred times.'

'But nobody could take the documents home,' said the colonel. 'Each new official must have found them in the proper file.'

The lawyer lost his patience.

'And moreover if those papers are removed from the Ministry now, they will have to wait for a new place on the rolls.'

'It doesn't matter,' the colonel said.

'It'll take centuries.'

'It doesn't matter. If you wait for the big things, you can wait for the little ones.'

He took a pad of lined paper, the pen, the inkwell, and a blotter to the little table in the living room, and left the bedroom door open in case he had to ask his wife anything. She was saying her beads.

'What's today's date?'

'October 27th.'

He wrote with a studious neatness, the hand that held the pen resting on the blotter, his spine straight to ease his breathing, as he'd been taught in school. The heat became unbearable in the closed living room. A drop of perspiration fell on the letter. The colonel picked it up on the blotter. Then he tried to erase the letters which had smeared but he smudged them. He didn't lose his patience. He wrote an asterisk and noted in the margin, 'acquired rights.' Then he read the whole paragraph.

'When was I put on the rolls?'

The woman didn't interrupt her prayer to think.

'August 12, 1949.'

A moment later it began to rain. The colonel filled a page with large doodlings which were a little childish, the same ones he learned in public school at Manaure. Then he wrote on a second sheet down to the middle, and he signed it.

He read the letter to his wife. She approved each sentence with a nod. When he finished reading, the colonel sealed the envelope and turned off the lamp.

'You could ask someone to type it for you.'

'No,' the colonel answered. 'I'm tired of going around asking favors.'

For half an hour he heard the rain against the palm roof. The town sank into the deluge. After curfew sounded, a leak began somewhere in the house.

'This should have been done a long time ago,' the woman said. 'It's always better to handle things oneself.'

'It's never too late,' the colonel said, paying attention

to the leak. 'Maybe all this will be settled when the mortgage on the house falls due.'

'In two years,' the woman said.

He lit the lamp to locate the leak in the living room. He put the rooster's can underneath it and returned to the bedroom, pursued by the metallic noise of the water in the empty can.

'It's possible that to save the interest on the money they'll settle it before January,' he said, and he convinced himself. 'By then, Agustín's year will be up and we can go to the movies.'

She laughed under her breath. 'I don't even remember the cartoons any more,' she said. 'They were showing *The Dead Man's Will*.'

'Was there a fight?'

'We never found out. The storm broke just when the ghost tried to rob the girl's necklace.'

The sound of the rain put them to sleep. The colonel felt a slight queasiness in his intestines. But he wasn't afraid. He was about to survive another October. He wrapped himself in a wool blanket, and for a moment heard the gravelly breathing of his wife – far away – drifting on another dream. Then he spoke, completely conscious.

The woman woke up.

'Who are you speaking to?'

'No one,' the colonel said. 'I was thinking that at the Macondo meeting we were right when we told Colonel Aureliano Buendía not to surrender. That's what started to ruin everything.'

It rained the whole week. The second of November – against the colonel's wishes – the woman took flowers to Agustín's grave. She returned from the cemetery and had another attack. It was a hard week. Harder than the four weeks of October which the colonel hadn't thought he'd survive. The doctor came to see the sick woman, and came out of the room shouting. 'With asthma like that, I'd be able to bury the whole town!' But he spoke to the colonel alone and prescribed a special diet.

The colonel also suffered a relapse. He strained for many hours in the privy, in an icy sweat, feeling as if he were rotting and that the flora in his vitals was falling to pieces. 'It's winter,' he repeated to himself patiently. 'Everything will be different when it stops raining.' And he really believed it, certain that he would be alive at the moment the letter arrived.

This time it was he who had to repair their household economy. He had to grit his teeth many times to ask for credit in the neighborhood stores. 'It's just until next week,' he would say, without being sure himself that it was true. 'It's a little money which should have arrived last Friday.' When her attack was over, the woman examined him in horror.

'You're nothing but skin and bones,' she said.

'I'm taking care of myself so I can sell myself,' the colonel said. 'I've already been hired by a clarinet factory.'

But in reality his hoping for the letter barely sustained him. Exhausted, his bones aching from sleeplessness, he couldn't attend to his needs and the rooster's at the same time. In the second half of November, he thought that the animal would die after two days without corn. Then he remembered a handful of beans which he had hung in the chimney in July. He opened the pods and put down a can of dry seeds for the rooster.

'Come here,' she said.

'Just a minute,' the colonel answered, watching the rooster's reaction. 'Beggars can't be choosers.'

He found his wife trying to sit up in bed. Her ravaged body gave off the aroma of medicinal herbs. She spoke her words, one by one, with calculated precision:

'Get rid of that rooster right now.'

The colonel had foreseen that moment. He had been waiting for it ever since the afternoon when his son was shot down, and he had decided to keep the rooster. He had had time to think.

'It's not worth it now,' he said. 'The fight will be in two months and then we'll be able to sell him at a better price.'

'It's not a question of the money,' the woman said. 'When the boys come, you'll tell them to take it away and do whatever they feel like with it.'

'It's for Agustín,' the colonel said, advancing his prepared argument. 'Remember his face when he came to tell us the rooster won.'

The woman, in fact, did think of her son.

'Those accursed roosters were his downfall!' she shouted. 'If he'd stayed home on January 3rd, his evil hour wouldn't have come.' She held out a skinny forefinger toward the door and exclaimed: 'It seems as if I can see him when he left with the rooster under his arm. I warned him not to go looking for trouble at the cockfights, and he smiled and told me: "Shut up; this afternoon we'll be rolling in money."'

She fell back exhausted. The colonel pushed her gently toward the pillow. His eyes fell upon other eyes exactly like his own. 'Try not to move,' he said, feeling her whistling within his own lungs. The woman fell into a momentary torpor. She closed her eyes. When she opened them again, her breathing seemed more even.

'It's because of the situation we're in,' she said. 'It's a sin to take the food out of our mouths to give it to a rooster.'

The colonel wiped her forehead with the sheet.

'Nobody dies in three months.'

'And what do we eat in the meantime?' the woman asked.

'I don't know,' the colonel said. 'But if we were going to die of hunger, we would have died already.'

The rooster was very much alive next to the empty can. When he saw the colonel, he emitted an almost human, guttural monologue and tossed his head back. He gave him a smile of complicity:

'Life is tough, pal.'

The colonel went into the street. He wandered about the town during the siesta, without thinking about anything, without even trying to convince himself that his problem had no solution. He walked through forgotten streets until he found he was exhausted. Then he returned to the house. The woman heard him come in and called him into the bedroom.

'What?'

She replied without looking at him.

'We can sell the clock.'

The colonel had thought of that. 'I'm sure Alvaro will give you forty pesos right on the spot,' said the woman.

'Think how quickly he bought the sewing machine.'

She was referring to the tailor whom Agustín had worked for.

'I could speak to him in the morning,' admitted the colonel.

'None of that "speak to him in the morning,"' she insisted. 'Take the clock to him this minute. You put it on the counter and you tell him, "Alvaro, I've brought this clock for you to buy from me." He'll understand immediately.'

The colonel felt ashamed.

'It's like walking around with the Holy Sepulcher,' he protested. 'If they see me in the street with a show-piece like that, Rafael Escalona will put me into one of his songs.'

But this time, too, his wife convinced him. She herself took down the clock, wrapped it in newspaper, and put it into his arms. 'Don't come back here without the forty pesos,' she said. The colonel went off to the tailor's with the package under his arm. He found Agustín's companions sitting in the doorway.

One of them offered him a seat. 'Thanks,' he said. 'I can't stay.' Alvaro came out of the shop. A piece of wet duck hung on a wire stretched between two hooks in the hall. He was a boy with a hard, angular body and wild eyes. He also invited him to sit down. The colonel felt comforted. He leaned the stool against the door-jamb and sat down to wait until Alvaro was alone to propose his deal. Suddenly he realized that he was surrounded by expressionless faces.

'I'm not interrupting?' he said.

They said he wasn't. One of them leaned toward him.

34

He said in a barely audible voice: 'Agustín wrote.'

The colonel observed the deserted street.

'What does he say?'

'The same as always.'

They gave him the clandestine sheet of paper. The colonel put it in his pants pocket. Then he kept silent, drumming on the package, until he realized that someone had noticed it. He stopped in suspense.

'What have you got there, colonel?'

The colonel avoided Hernán's penetrating green eyes.

'Nothing,' he lied. 'I'm taking my clock to the German to have him fix it for me.'

'Don't be silly, colonel,' said Hernán, trying to take the package. 'Wait and I'll look at it.'

The colonel held back. He didn't say anything, but his eyelids turned purple. The others insisted.

'Let him, colonel. He knows mechanical things.'

'I just don't want to bother him.'

'Bother, it's no bother,' Hernán argued. He seized the clock. 'The German will get ten pesos out of you and it'll be the same as it is now.'

Hernán went into the tailor shop with the clock. Alvaro was sewing on a machine. At the back, beneath a guitar hanging on a nail, a girl was sewing buttons on. There was a sign tacked up over the guitar: 'TALKING POLITICS FORBIDDEN.' Outside, the colonel felt as if his body were superfluous. He rested his feet on the rail of the stool.

'Goddamn it, colonel.'

He was startled. 'No need to swear,' he said.

Alfonso adjusted his eyeglasses on his nose to examine the colonel's shoes.

'It's because of your shoes,' he said. 'You've got on some goddamn new shoes.'

'But you can say that without swearing,' the colonel said, and showed the soles of his patent-leather shoes. 'These monstrosities are forty years old, and it's the first time they've ever heard anyone swear.'

'All done,' shouted Hernán, inside, just as the clock's bell rang. In the neighboring house, a woman pounded on the partition; she shouted: 'Let that guitar alone! Agustín's year isn't up yet.'

Someone guffawed.

'It's a clock.'

Hernán came out with the package.

'It wasn't anything,' he said. 'If you like I'll go home with you to level it.'

The colonel refused his offer.

'How much do I owe you?'

'Don't worry about it, colonel,' replied Hernán, taking his place in the group. 'In January, the rooster will pay for it.'

The colonel now found the chance he was looking for.

'I'll make you a deal,' he said.

'What?'

'I'll give you the rooster.' He examined the circle of faces. 'I'll give the rooster to all of you.'

Hernán looked at him in confusion.

'I'm too old now for that,' the colonel continued. He gave his voice a convincing severity. 'It's too much responsibility for me. For days now I've had the impression that the animal is dying.'

'Don't worry about it, colonel,' Alfonso said. 'The

trouble is that the rooster is molting now. He's got a fever in his quills.'

'He'll be better next month,' Hernán said.

'I don't want him anyway,' the colonel said.

Hernán's pupils bore into his.

'Realize how things are, colonel,' he insisted. 'The main thing is for you to be the one who puts Agustín's rooster into the ring.'

The colonel thought about it. 'I realize,' he said. 'That's why I've kept him until now.' He clenched his teeth, and felt he could go on: 'The trouble is there are still two months.'

Hernán was the one who understood.

'If it's only because of that, there's no problem,' he said.

And he proposed his formula. The other accepted. At dusk, when he entered the house with the package under his arm, his wife was chagrined.

'Nothing?' she asked.

'Nothing,' the colonel answered. 'But now it doesn't matter. The boys will take over feeding the rooster.'

'Wait and I'll lend you an umbrella, friend.'

Sabas opened a cupboard in the office wall. He uncovered a jumbled interior: riding boots piled up, stirrups and reins, and an aluminum pail full of riding spurs. Hanging from the upper part, half a dozen umbrellas and a lady's parasol. The colonel was thinking of the debris from some catastrophe.

'Thanks, friend,' the colonel said, leaning on the window. 'I prefer to wait for it to clear.' Sabas didn't close the cupboard. He settled down at the desk within range of the electric fan. Then he took a little hypodermic syringe wrapped in cotton out of the drawer. The colonel observed the grayish almond trees through the rain. It was an empty afternoon.

'The rain is different from this window,' he said. 'It's as if it were raining in another town.'

'Rain is rain from whatever point,' replied Sabas. He put the syringe on to boil on the glass desk top. 'This town stinks.'

The colonel shrugged his shoulders. He walked toward the middle of the office: a green-tiled room with furniture upholstered in brightly colored fabrics. At the back, piled up in disarray, were sacks of salt, honeycombs, and riding saddles. Sabas followed him with a completely vacant stare.

'If I were in your shoes I wouldn't think that way,' said the colonel.

He sat down and crossed his legs, his calm gaze fixed on the man leaning over his desk. A small man, corpulent, but with flaccid flesh, he had the sadness of a toad in his eyes.

'Have the doctor look at you, friend,' said Sabas. 'You've been a little sad since the day of the funeral.'

The colonel raised his head.

'I'm perfectly well,' he said.

Sabas waited for the syringe to boil. 'I wish I could say the same,' he complained. 'You're lucky because you've got a cast-iron stomach.' He contemplated the hairy backs of his hands which were dotted with dark blotches. He wore a ring with a black stone next to his wedding band.

'That's right,' the colonel admitted.

Sabas called his wife through the door between the office and the rest of the house. Then he began a painful explanation of his diet. He took a little bottle out of his shirt pocket and put a white pill the size of a pea on the desk.

'It's torture to go around with this everyplace,' he said. 'It's like carrying death in your pocket.'

The colonel approached the desk. He examined the pill in the palm of his hand until Sabas invited him to taste it.

'It's to sweeten coffee,' he explained. 'It's sugar, but without sugar.'

'Of course,' the colonel said, his saliva impregnated with a sad sweetness. 'It's something like a ringing but without bells.'

Sabas put his elbows on the desk with his face in his hands after his wife gave him the injection. The colonel didn't know what to do with his body. The woman unplugged the electric fan, put it on top of the safe, and then went to the cupboard.

'Umbrellas have something to do with death,' she said.

The colonel paid no attention to her. He had left his house at four to wait for the mail, but the rain made him take refuge in Sabas's office. It was still raining when the launches whistled.

'Everybody says death is a woman,' the woman continued. She was fat, taller than her husband, and had a hairy mole on her upper lip. Her way of speaking reminded one of the hum of the electric fan. 'But I don't think it's a woman,' she said. She closed the cupboard and looked into the colonel's eyes again.

'I think it's an animal with claws.'

'That's possible,' the colonel admitted. 'At times very strange things happen.'

He thought of the postmaster jumping onto the launch in an oilskin slicker. A month had passed since he had changed lawyers. He was entitled to expect a reply. Sabas's wife kept speaking about death until she noticed the colonel's absent-minded expression.

'Friend,' she said. 'You must be worried.'

The colonel sat up.

'That's right friend,' he lied. 'I'm thinking that it's five already and the rooster hasn't had his injection.'

She was confused.

'An injection for a rooster, as if he were a human being!' she shouted. 'That's a sacrilege.'

Sabas couldn't stand any more. He raised his flushed face.

'Close your mouth for a minute,' he ordered his wife. And in fact she did raise her hands to her mouth. 'You've been bothering my friend for half an hour with your foolishness.'

'Not at all,' the colonel protested.

The woman slammed the door. Sabas dried his neck with a handkerchief soaked in lavender. The colonel approached the window. It was raining steadily. A long-legged chicken was crossing the deserted plaza.

'Is it true the rooster's getting injections?'

'True,' said the colonel. 'His training begins next week.'

'That's madness,' said Sabas. 'Those things are not for you.'

'I agree,' said the colonel. 'But that's no reason to wring his neck.'

'That's just idiotic stubbornness,' said Sabas, turning toward the window. The colonel heard him sigh with the breath of a bellows. His friend's eyes made him feel pity.

'It's never too late for anything,' the colonel said.

'Don't be unreasonable,' insisted Sabas. 'It's a two-edged deal. On one side you get rid of that headache, and on the other you can put nine hundred pesos in your pocket.'

'Nine hundred pesos!' the colonel exclaimed.

'Nine hundred pesos.'

The colonel visualized the figure.

'You think they'd give a fortune like that for the rooster?'

'I don't think,' Sabas answered. 'I'm absolutely sure.'

It was the largest sum the colonel had had in his head since he had returned the revolution's funds. When he left Sabas's office, he felt a strong wrenching in his gut, but he was aware that this time it wasn't because of the weather. At the post office he headed straight for the postmaster:

'I'm expecting an urgent letter,' he said. 'It's air mail.'

The postmaster looked in the cubbyholes. When he finished reading, he put the letters back in the proper box but he didn't say anything. He dusted off his hand and turned a meaningful look on the colonel.

'It was supposed to come today for sure,' the colonel said.

The postmaster shrugged.

'The only thing that comes for sure is death, colonel.'

His wife received him with a dish of corn mush. He ate

it in silence with long pauses for thought between each spoonful. Seated opposite him, the woman noticed that something had changed in his face.

'What's the matter?' she asked.

'I'm thinking about the employee that pension depends on,' the colonel lied. 'In fifty years, we'll be peacefully six feet under, while that poor man will be killing himself every Friday waiting for his retirement pension.'

'That's a bad sign,' the woman said. 'It means that you're beginning to resign yourself already.' She went on eating her mush. But a moment later she realized that her husband was still far away.

'Now, what you should do is enjoy the mush.'

'It's very good,' the colonel said. 'Where'd it come from?'

'From the rooster,' the woman answered. 'The boys brought him so much corn that he decided to share it with us. That's life.'

'That's right.' The colonel sighed. 'Life is the best thing that's ever been invented.'

He looked at the rooster tied to the leg of the stove and this time he seemed a different animal. The woman also looked at him.

'This afternoon I had to chase the children out with a stick,' she said. 'They brought an old hen to breed her with the rooster.'

'It's not the first time,' the colonel said. 'That's the same thing they did in those towns with Colonel Aureliano Buendía. They brought him little girls to breed with.'

She got a kick out of the joke. The rooster produced a guttural noise which sounded in the hall like quiet human conversation. 'Sometimes I think that animal is going to talk,' the woman said. The colonel looked at him again.

'He's worth his weight in gold,' he said. He made some calculations while he sipped a spoonful of mush. 'He'll feed us for three years.'

'You can't eat hope,' the woman said.

'You can't eat it, but it sustains you,' the colonel replied. 'It's something like my friend Sabas's miraculous pills.'

He slept poorly that night trying to erase the figures from his mind. The following day at lunch, the woman served two plates of mush, and ate hers with her head lowered, without saying a word. The colonel felt himself catching her dark mood.

'What's the matter?'

'Nothing,' the woman said.

He had the impression that this time it had been her turn to lie. He tried to comfort her. But the woman persisted.

'It's nothing unusual,' she said. 'I was thinking that the man has been dead for two months, and I still haven't been to see the family.'

So she went to see them that night. The colonel accompanied her to the dead man's house, and then headed for the movie theater, drawn by the music coming over the loudspeakers. Seated at the door of his office, Father Ángel was watching the entrance to find out who was attending the show despite his twelve warnings. The flood of light, the strident music, and the shouts of the children erected a physical resistance in the area. One of the children threatened the colonel with a wooden rifle.

'What's new with the rooster, colonel?' he said in an authoritative voice.

The colonel put his hands up.

'He's still around.'

A four-color poster covered the entire front of the theater: *Midnight Virgin*. She was a woman in an evening gown, with one leg bared up to the thigh. The colonel continued wandering around the neighborhood until distant thunder and lightning began. Then he went back for his wife.

She wasn't at the dead man's house. Nor at home. The colonel reckoned that there was little time left before curfew, but the clock had stopped. He waited, feeling the storm advance on the town. He was getting ready to go out again when his wife arrived.

He took the rooster into the bedroom. She changed her clothes and went to take a drink of water in the living room just as the colonel finished winding the clock, and was waiting for curfew to blow in order to set it.

'Where were you?' the colonel asked.

'Roundabout,' the woman answered. She put the glass on the washstand without looking at her husband and returned to the bedroom. 'No one thought it was going to rain so soon.' The colonel made no comment. When curfew blew, he set the clock at eleven, closed the case, and put the chair back in its place. He found his wife saying her rosary.

'You haven't answered my question,' the colonel said.

'What?'

'Where were you?'

44

'I stayed around there talking,' she said. 'It had been so long since I'd been out of the house.'

The colonel hung up his hammock. He locked the house and fumigated the room. Then he put the lamp on the floor and lay down.

'I understand,' he said sadly. 'The worst of a bad situation is that it makes us tell lies.'

She let out a long sigh.

'I was with Father Ángel,' she said. 'I went to ask him for a loan on our wedding rings.'

'And what did he tell you?'

'That it's a sin to barter with sacred things.'

She went on talking under her mosquito netting. 'Two days ago I tried to sell the clock,' she said. 'No one is interested because they're selling modern clocks with luminous numbers on the installment plan. You can see the time in the dark.' The colonel acknowledged that forty years of shared living, of shared hunger, of shared suffering, had not been enough for him to come to know his wife. He felt that something had also grown old in their love.

'They don't want the picture, either,' she said. 'Almost everybody has the same one. I even went to the Turk's.'

The colonel felt bitter.

'So now everyone knows we're starving.'

'I'm tired,' the woman said. 'Men don't understand problems of the household. Several times I've had to put stones on to boil so the neighbors wouldn't know that we often go for many days without putting on the pot.'

The colonel felt offended.

45

'That's really a humiliation,' he said.

The woman got out from under the mosquito netting and went to the hammock. 'I'm ready to give up affectation and pretense in this house,' she said. Her voice began to darken with rage. 'I'm fed up with resignation and dignity.'

The colonel didn't move a muscle.

'Twenty years of waiting for the little colored birds which they promised you after every election, and all we've got out of it is a dead son,' she went on. 'Nothing but a dead son.'

The colonel was used to that sort of recrimination.

'We did our duty.'

'And they did theirs by making a thousand pesos a month in the Senate for twenty years,' the woman answered. 'There's my friend Sabas with a two-story house that isn't big enough to keep all his money in, a man who came to this town selling medicines with a snake curled around his neck.'

'But he's dying of diabetes,' the colonel said.

'And you're dying of hunger,' the woman said. 'You should realize that you can't eat dignity.'

The lightning interrupted her. The thunder exploded in the street, entered the bedroom, and went rolling under the bed like a heap of stones. The woman jumped toward the mosquito netting for her rosary.

The colonel smiled.

'That's what happens to you for not holding your tongue,' he said. 'I've always said that God is on my side.'

But in reality he felt embittered. A moment later he put out the light and sank into thought in a darkness rent by the lightning. He remembered Macondo. The colonel had waited ten years for the promises of Neerlandia to be fulfilled. In the drowsiness of the siesta he saw a yellow, dusty train pull in, with men and women and animals suffocating from the heat, piled up even on the roofs of the cars. It was the banana fever.

In twenty-four hours they had transformed the town. 'I'm leaving,' the colonel said then. 'The odor of the banana is eating at my insides.' And he left Macondo on the return train, Wednesday, June 27, 1906 at 2:18 p.m. It took him nearly half a century to realize that he hadn't had a moment's peace since the surrender at Neerlandia.

He opened his eyes.

'Then there's no need to think about it any more,' he said.

'What?'

'The problem of the rooster,' the colonel said. 'Tomorrow I'll sell it to my friend Sabas for nine hundred pesos.'

The howls of the castrated animals, fused with Sabas's shouting, came through the office window. If he doesn't come in ten minutes I'll leave, the colonel promised himself after two hours of waiting. But he waited twenty minutes more. He was getting set to leave when Sabas entered the office followed by a group of workers. He passed back and forth in front of the colonel without looking at him.

'Are you waiting for me, friend?'

'Yes, friend,' the colonel said. 'But if you're very busy, I can come back later.'

Sabas didn't hear him from the other side of the door.

'I'll be right back,' he said.

Noon was stifling. The office shone with the shimmering of the street. Dulled by the heat, the colonel involuntarily closed his eyes and at once began to dream of his wife. Sabas's wife came in on tiptoe.

'Don't wake up, friend,' she said. 'I'm going to draw the blinds because this office is an inferno.'

The colonel followed her with a blank look. She spoke in the shadow when she closed the window.

'Do you dream often?'

'Sometimes,' replied the colonel, ashamed of having fallen asleep. 'Almost always I dream that I'm getting tangled up in spider webs.'

'I have nightmares every night,' the woman said. 'Now I've got it in my head to find out who those unknown people are whom one meets in one's dreams.'

She plugged in the fan. 'Last week a woman appeared at the head of my bed,' she said. 'I managed to ask her who she was and she replied, "I am the woman who died in this room twelve years ago."'

'But the house was built barely two years ago,' the colonel said.

'That's right,' the woman said. 'That means that even the dead make mistakes.'

The hum of the fan solidified the shadow. The colonel felt impatient, tormented by sleepiness and by the rambling woman who went directly from dreams to the mystery of the reincarnation. He was waiting for a pause to say goodbye when Sabas entered the office with his foreman.

'I've warmed up your soup four times,' the woman said.

'Warm it up ten times if you like,' said Sabas. 'But stop nagging me now.'

He opened the safe and gave his foreman a roll of bills together with a list of instructions. The foreman opened the blinds to count the money. Sabas saw the colonel at the back of the office but didn't show any reaction. He kept talking with the foreman. The colonel straightened up at the point when the two men were getting ready to leave the office again. Sabas stopped before opening the door.

'What can I do for you, friend?'

The colonel saw that the foreman was looking at him.

'Nothing, friend,' he said. 'I just wanted to talk to you.'

'Make it fast, whatever it is,' said Sabas. 'I don't have a minute to spare.'

He hesitated with his hand resting on the doorknob. The colonel felt the five longest seconds of his life passing. He clenched his teeth.

'It's about the rooster,' he murmured.

Then Sabas finished opening the door. 'The question of the rooster,' he repeated, smiling, and pushed the foreman toward the hall. 'The sky is falling in and my friend is worrying about that rooster.' And then, addressing the colonel:

'Very well, friend. I'll be right back.'

The colonel stood motionless in the middle of the office until he could no longer hear the footsteps of the two men at the end of the hall. Then he went out to

49

walk around the town which was paralyzed in its Sunday siesta. There was no one at the tailor's. The doctor's office was closed. No one was watching the goods set out at the Syrians' stalls. The river was a sheet of steel. A man at the waterfront was sleeping across four oil drums, his face protected from the sun by a hat. The colonel went home, certain that he was the only thing moving in town.

His wife was waiting for him with a complete lunch.

'I bought it on credit; promised to pay first thing tomorrow,' she explained.

During lunch, the colonel told her the events of the last three hours. She listened to him impatiently.

'The trouble is you lack character,' she said finally. 'You present yourself as if you were begging alms when you ought to go there with your head high and take our friend aside and say, "Friend, I've decided to sell you the rooster."'

'Life is a breeze the way you tell it,' the colonel said.

She assumed an energetic attitude. That morning she had put the house in order and was dressed very strangely, in her husband's old shoes, an oilcloth apron, and a rag tied around her head with two knots at the ears. 'You haven't the slightest sense for business,' she said. 'When you go to sell something, you have to put on the same face as when you go to buy.'

The colonel found something amusing in her figure.

'Stay just the way you are,' he interrupted her, smiling. 'You're identical to the little Quaker Oats man.'

She took the rag off her head.

'I'm speaking seriously,' she said. 'I'm going to take the rooster to our friend right now, and I'll bet whatever you want that I come back inside of half an hour with the nine hundred pesos.'

'You've got zeros on the brain,' the colonel said. 'You're already betting with the money from the rooster.'

It took a lot of trouble for him to dissuade her. She had spent the morning mentally organizing the budget for the next three years without their Friday agony. She had made a list of the essentials they needed, without forgetting a pair of new shoes for the colonel. She set aside a place in the bedroom for the mirror. The momentary frustration of her plans left her with a confused sensation of shame and resentment.

She took a short siesta. When she got up, the colonel was sitting in the patio.

'Now what are you doing?' she asked.

'I'm thinking,' the colonel said.

'Then the problem is solved. We will be able to count on that money fifty years from now.'

But in reality the colonel had decided to sell the rooster that very afternoon. He thought of Sabas, alone in his office, preparing himself for his daily injection in front of the electric fan. He had his answer ready.

'Take the rooster,' his wife advised him as he went out. 'Seeing him in the flesh will work a miracle.'

The colonel objected. She followed him to the front door with desperate anxiety.

'It doesn't matter if the whole army is in the office,' she said. 'You grab him by the arm and don't let him move until he gives you the nine hundred pesos.'

'They'll think we're planning a hold-up.'

She paid no attention.

'Remember that you are the owner of the rooster,'

she insisted. 'Remember that you are the one who's going to do him the favor.'

'All right.'

Sabas was in the bedroom with the doctor. 'Now's your chance, friend,' his wife said to the colonel. 'The doctor is getting him ready to travel to the ranch, and he's not coming back until Thursday.' The colonel struggled with two opposing forces: in spite of his determination to sell the rooster, he wished he had arrived an hour later and missed Sabas.

'I can wait,' he said.

But the woman insisted. She led him to the bedroom where her husband was seated on the throne-like bed, in his underwear, his colorless eyes fixed on the doctor. The colonel waited until the doctor had heated the glass tube with the patient's urine, sniffed the odor, and made an approving gesture to Sabas.

'We'll have to shoot him,' the doctor said, turning to the colonel. 'Diabetes is too slow for finishing off the wealthy.'

'You've already done your best with your damned insulin injections,' said Sabas, and he gave a jump on his flaccid buttocks. 'But I'm a hard nut to crack.' And then, to the colonel:

'Come in, friend. When I went to look for you this afternoon, I couldn't even see your hat.'

'I don't wear one, so I won't have to take if off for anyone.'

Sabas began to get dressed. The doctor put a glass tube with a blood sample in his jacket pocket. Then he straightened out the things in his bag. The colonel thought he was getting ready to leave.

'If I were in your shoes, I'd send my friend a bill for a hundred thousand pesos, doctor,' the colonel said. 'That way he wouldn't be so worried.'

'I've already suggested that to him, but for a million,' the doctor said. 'Poverty is the best cure for diabetes.'

'Thanks for the prescription,' said Sabas, trying to stuff his voluminous belly into his riding breeches. 'But I won't accept it, to save you from the catastrophe of becoming rich.' The doctor saw his own teeth reflected in the little chromed lock of his bag. He looked at the clock without showing impatience. Sabas, putting on his boots, suddenly turned to the colonel: 'Well, friend, what's happening with the rooster?'

The colonel realized that the doctor was also waiting for his answer. He clenched his teeth.

'Nothing, friend,' he murmured. 'I've come to sell him to you.'

Sabas finished putting on his boots.

'Fine, my friend,' he said without emotion. 'It's the most sensible thing that could have occurred to you.'

'I'm too old now for these complications,' the colonel said to justify himself before the doctor's impenetrable expression. 'If I were twenty years younger it would be different.'

'You'll always be twenty years younger,' the doctor replied.

The colonel regained his breath. He waited for Sabas to say something more, but he didn't. Sabas put on a leather zippered jacket and got ready to leave the bedroom.

'If you like, we'll talk about it next week, friend,' the colonel said.

'That's what I was going to say,' said Sabas. 'I have a

customer who might give you four hundred pesos. But we have to wait till Thursday.'

'How much?' the doctor asked.

'Four hundred pesos.'

'I had heard someone say that he was worth a lot more,' the doctor said.

'You were talking in terms of nine hundred pesos,' the colonel said, backed by the doctor's perplexity. 'He's the best rooster in the whole province.'

Sabas answered the doctor.

'At some other time, anyone would have paid a thousand,' he explained. 'But now no one dares pit a good rooster. There's always the danger he'll come out of the pit shot to death.' He turned to the colonel, feigning disappointment: 'That's what I wanted to tell you, friend.'

The colonel nodded.

'Fine,' he said.

He followed him down the hall. The doctor stayed in the living room, detained by Sabas's wife, who asked him for a remedy 'for those things which come over one suddenly and which one doesn't know what they are.' The colonel waited for him in the office. Sabas opened the safe, stuffed money into all his pockets, and held out four bills to the colonel.

'There's sixty pesos, friend,' he said. 'When the rooster is sold we'll settle up.'

The colonel walked with the doctor past the stalls at the waterfront, which were beginning to revive in the cool of the afternoon. A barge loaded with sugar cane was moving down the thread of current. The colonel found the doctor strangely impervious.

'And you, how are you, doctor?'

The doctor shrugged.

'As usual,' he said. 'I think I need a doctor.'

'It's the winter,' the colonel said. 'It eats away my insides.'

The doctor examined him with a look absolutely devoid of any professional interest. In succession he greeted the Syrians seated at the doors of their shops. At the door of the doctor's office, the colonel expressed his opinion of the sale of the rooster.

'I couldn't do anything else,' he explained. 'That animal feeds on human flesh.'

'The only animal who feeds on human flesh is Sabas,' the doctor said. 'I'm sure he'd resell the rooster for the nine hundred pesos.'

'You think so?'

'I'm sure of it,' the doctor said. 'It's as sweet a deal as his famous patriotic pact with the mayor.'

The colonel refused to believe it. 'My friend made that pact to save his skin,' he said. 'That's how he could stay in town.'

'And that's how he could buy the property of his fellow-partisans whom the mayor kicked out at half their price,' the doctor replied. He knocked on the door, since he didn't find his keys in his pockets. Then he faced the colonel's disbelief.

'Don't be so naïve,' he said. 'Sabas is much more interested in money than in his own skin.'

The colonel's wife went shopping that night. He accompanied her to the Syrians' stalls, pondering the doctor's revelations.

'Find the boys immediately and tell them that the

rooster is sold,' she told him. 'We mustn't leave them with any hopes.'

'The rooster won't be sold until my friend Sabas comes back,' the colonel answered.

He found Alvaro playing roulette in the pool hall. The place was sweltering on Sunday night. The heat seemed more intense because of the vibrations of the radio turned up full blast. The colonel amused himself with the brightly colored numbers painted on a large black oilcloth cover and lit by an oil lantern placed on a box in the center of the table. Alvaro insisted on losing on twenty-three. Following the game over his shoulder, the colonel observed that the eleven turned up four times in nine spins.

'Bet on eleven,' he whispered into Alvaro's ear. 'It's the one coming up most.'

Alvaro examined the table. He didn't bet on the next spin. He took some money out of his pants pocket, and with it a sheet of paper. He gave the paper to the colonel under the table.

'It's from Agustín,' he said.

The colonel put the clandestine note in his pocket. Alvaro bet heavily on the eleven.

'Start with just a little,' the colonel said.

'It may be a good hunch,' Alvaro replied. A group of neighboring players took their bets off the other numbers and bet on eleven after the enormous colored wheel had already begun to turn. The colonel felt oppressed. For the first time he felt the fascination, agitation, and bitterness of gambling.

The five won.

'I'm sorry,' the colonel said, ashamed, and, with an

irresistible feeling of guilt, followed the little wooden rake which pulled in Alvaro's money. 'That's what I get for butting into what doesn't concern me.'

Alvaro smiled without looking at him.

'Don't worry, colonel. Trust to love.'

The trumpets playing a mambo were suddenly interrupted. The gamblers scattered with their hands in the air. The colonel felt the dry snap, articulate and cold, of a rifle being cocked behind his back. He realized that he had been caught fatally in a police raid with the clandestine paper in his pocket. He turned halfway around without raising his hands. And then he saw, close up, for the first time in his life, the man who had shot his son. The man was directly in front of him, with his rifle barrel aimed at the colonel's belly. He was small, Indian-looking, with weather-beaten skin, and his breath smelled like a child's. The colonel gritted his teeth and gently pushed the rifle barrel away with the tips of his fingers.

'Excuse me,' he said.

He confronted two round little bat eyes. In an instant, he felt himself being swallowed up by those eyes, crushed, digested, and expelled immediately.

'You may go, colonel.'

He didn't need to open the window to tell it was December. He knew it in his bones when he was cutting up the fruit for the rooster's breakfast in the kitchen. Then he opened the door and the sight of the patio confirmed his feeling. It was a marvelous patio, with the grass and the trees, and the cubicle with the privy floating in the clear air, one millimeter above the ground.

His wife stayed in bed until nine. When she appeared in the kitchen, the colonel had already straightened up the house and was talking to the children in a circle around the rooster. She had to make a detour to get to the stove.

'Get out of the way!' she shouted. She glowered in the animal's direction. 'I don't know when I'll ever get rid of the evil-omened bird.'

The colonel regarded his wife's mood over the rooster. Nothing about the rooster deserved resentment. He was ready for training. His neck and his feathered purple thighs, his saw-toothed crest: the animal had taken on a slender figure, a defenseless air.

'Lean out the window and forget the rooster,' the colonel said when the children left. 'On mornings like this, one feels like having a picture taken.'

She leaned out the window but her face betrayed no emotion. 'I would like to plant the roses,' she said, returning to the stove. The colonel hung the mirror on the hook to shave.

'If you want to plant the roses, go ahead,' he said.

He tried to make his movements match those in the mirror.

'The pigs eat them up,' she said.

'All the better,' the colonel said. 'Pigs fattened on roses ought to taste very good.'

He looked for his wife in the mirror and noticed that she still had the same expression. By the light of the fire her face seemed to be formed of the same material as the stove. Without noticing, his eyes fixed on her, the colonel continued shaving himself by touch as he had done for many years. The woman thought, in a long silence.

'But I don't want to plant them,' she said.

'Fine,' said the colonel. 'Then don't plant them.'

He felt well. December had shriveled the flora in his gut. He suffered a disappointment that morning trying to put on his new shoes. But after trying several times he realized that it was a wasted effort, and put on his patent-leather ones. His wife noticed the change.

'If you don't put on the new ones you'll never break them in,' she said.

'They're shoes for a cripple,' the colonel protested. 'They ought to sell shoes that have already been worn for a month.'

He went into the street stimulated by the presentiment that the letter would arrive that afternoon. Since it still was not time for the launches, he waited for Sabas in his office. But they informed him that he wouldn't be back until Monday. He didn't lose his patience despite not having foreseen this setback. 'Sooner or later he has to come back,' he told himself, and he headed for the harbor; it was a marvelous moment, a moment of still-unblemished clarity.

'The whole year ought to be December,' he murmured, seated in the store of Moses the Syrian. 'One feels as if he were made of glass.'

Moses the Syrian had to make an effort to translate the idea into his almost forgotten Arabic. He was a placid Oriental, encased up to his ears in smooth, stretched skin, and he had the clumsy movements of a drowned man. In fact, he seemed as if he had just been rescued from the water.

'That's the way it was before,' he said. 'If it were the same now, I would be eight hundred and ninety-seven years old. And you?'

'Seventy-five,' said the colonel, his eyes pursuing the postmaster. Only then did he discover the circus. He recognized the patched tent on the roof of the mail boat amid a pile of colored objects. For a second he lost the postmaster while he looked for the wild animals among the crates piled up on the other launches. He didn't find them.

'It's a circus,' he said. 'It's the first one that's come in ten years.'

Moses the Syrian verified his report. He spoke to his wife in a pidgin of Arabic and Spanish. She replied from the back of the store. He made a comment to himself, and then translated his worry for the colonel.

'Hide your cat, colonel. The boys will steal it to sell it to the circus.'

The colonel was getting ready to follow the postmaster.

'It's not a wild-animal show,' he said.

'It doesn't matter,' the Syrian replied. 'The tightrope walkers eat cats so they won't break their bones.'

He followed the postmaster through the stalls at the waterfront to the plaza. There the loud clamor from the cockfight took him by surprise. A passer-by said something to him about his rooster. Only then did he remember that this was the day set for the trials.

He passed the post office. A moment later he had sunk into the turbulent atmosphere of the pit. He saw his rooster in the middle of the pit, alone, defenseless, his spurs wrapped in rags, with something like fear visible in the trembling of his feet. His adversary was a sad ashen rooster.

The colonel felt no emotion. There was a succession of identical attacks. A momentary engagement of feathers and feet and necks in the middle of an enthusiastic ovation. Knocked against the planks of the barrier, the adversary did a somersault and returned to the attack. His rooster didn't attack. He rebuffed every attack, and landed again in exactly the same spot. But now his feet weren't trembling.

Hernán jumped the barrier, picked him up with both hands, and showed him to the crowd in the stands. There was a frenetic explosion of applause and shouting. The colonel noticed the disproportion between the enthusiasm of the applause and the intensity of the fight. It seemed to him a farce to which – voluntarily and consciously – the roosters had also lent themselves.

Impelled by a slightly disdainful curiosity, he examined the circular pit. An excited crowd was hurtling down the stands toward the pit. The colonel observed the confusion of hot, anxious, terribly alive faces. They were new people. All the new people in town. He relived – with foreboding – an instant which had been erased on the edge of his memory. Then he leaped the barrier, made his way through the packed crowd in the pit, and confronted Hernán's calm eyes. They looked at each other without blinking.

'Good afternoon, colonel.'

The colonel took the rooster away from him. 'Good afternoon,' he muttered. And he said nothing more because the warm deep throbbing of the animal made him shudder. He thought that he had never had such an alive thing in his hands before.

'You weren't at home,' Hernán said, confused.

A new ovation interrupted him. The colonel felt intimidated. He made his way again, without looking at anybody, stunned by the applause and the shouts, and went into the street with his rooster under his arm.

The whole town – the lower-class people – came out to watch him go by followed by the school children. A gigantic negro standing on a table with a snake wrapped around his neck was selling medicine without a license at a corner of the plaza. A large group returning from the harbor had stopped to listen to his spiel. But when the colonel passed with the rooster, their attention shifted to him. The way home had never been so long.

He had no regrets. For a long time the town had lain in a sort of stupor, ravaged by ten years of history. That afternoon – another Friday without a letter – the people had awakened. The colonel remembered another era. He saw himself with his wife and his son watching under an umbrella a show which was not interrupted despite the rain. He remembered the party's leaders, scrupulously groomed, fanning themselves to the beat of the music in the patio of his house. He almost relived the painful resonance of the bass drum in his intestines.

He walked along the street parallel to the harbor and there, too, found the tumultuous Election Sunday crowd of long ago. They were watching the circus unloading. From inside a tent, a woman shouted something about the rooster. He continued home, self-absorbed, still hearing scattered voices, as if the remnants of the ovation in the pit were pursuing him.

At the door he addressed the children: 'Everyone go home,' he said. 'Anyone who comes in will leave with a hiding.'

He barred the door and went straight into the kitchen. His wife came out of the bedroom choking.

'They took it by force,' she said, sobbing. 'I told them that the rooster would not leave this house while I was alive.' The colonel tied the rooster to the leg of the stove. He changed the water in the can, pursued by his wife's frantic voice.

'They said they would take it over our dead bodies,' she said. 'They said the rooster didn't belong to us but to the whole town.'

Only when he finished with the rooster did the colonel turn to the contorted face of his wife. He discovered, without surprise, that it produced neither remorse nor compassion in him.

'They did the right thing,' he said quietly. And then looking through his pockets, he added with a sort of bottomless sweetness: 'The rooster's not for sale.'

She followed him to the bedroom. She felt him to be completely human, but untouchable, as if she were seeing him on a movie screen. The colonel took a roll of bills out of the closet, added what he had in his pockets to it, counted the total, and put it back in the closet.

'There are twenty-nine pesos to return to my friend Sabas,' he said. 'He'll get the rest when the pension arrives.'

'And if it doesn't arrive?' the woman asked.

'It will.'

'But if it doesn't?'

'Well, then, he won't get paid.'

He found his new shoes under the bed. He went back to the closet for the box, cleaned the soles with a rag, and put the shoes in the box, just as his wife had brought them Sunday night. She didn't move.

'The shoes go back,' the colonel said. 'That's thirteen pesos more for my friend.'

'They won't take them back,' she said.

'They have to take them back,' the colonel replied. 'I've only put them on twice.'

'The Turks don't understand such things,' the woman said.

'They have to understand.'

'And if they don't?'

'Well, then, they don't.'

They went to bed without eating. The colonel waited for his wife to finish her rosary to turn out the lamp. But he couldn't sleep. He heard the bells for the movie classifications, and almost at once – three hours later – the curfew. The gravelly breathing of his wife became anguished with the chilly night air. The colonel still had his eyes open when she spoke to him in a calm, conciliatory voice: 'You're awake.'

'Yes.'

'Try to listen to reason,' the woman said. 'Talk to my friend Sabas tomorrow.'

'He's not coming back until Monday.'

'Better,' said the woman. 'That way you'll have three days to think about what you're going to say.'

'There's nothing to think about,' the colonel said.

A pleasant coolness had taken the place of the viscous air of October. The colonel recognized December again in the timetable of the plovers. When it struck two, he still hadn't been able to fall asleep. But he knew that his wife was also awake. He tried to change his position in the hammock.

'You can't sleep,' the woman said.

'No.'

She thought for a moment.

'We're in no condition to do that,' she said. 'Just think how much four hundred pesos in one lump sum is.'

'It won't be long now till the pension comes,' the colonel said.

'You've been saying the same thing for fifteen years.'

'That's why,' the colonel said. 'It can't be much longer now.'

She was silent. But when she spoke again, it didn't seem to the colonel as if any time had passed at all.

'I have the impression the money will never arrive,' the woman said.

'It will.'

'And if it doesn't?'

He couldn't find his voice to answer. At the first crowing of the rooster he was struck by reality, but he sank back again into a dense, safe, remorseless sleep. When he awoke, the sun was already high in the sky. His wife was sleeping. The colonel methodically repeated his morning activities, two hours behind schedule, and waited for his wife to eat breakfast.

She was uncommunicative when she awoke. They said good morning, and they sat down to eat in silence. The colonel sipped a cup of black coffee and had a piece of cheese and a sweet roll. He spent the whole morning in the tailor shop. At one o'clock he returned home and found his wife mending clothes among the begonias.

'It's lunchtime,' he said.

'There is no lunch.'

He shrugged. He tried to block up the holes in the patio wall to prevent the children coming into the kitchen. When he came back into the hall, lunch was on the table.

During the course of lunch, the colonel realized that his wife was making an effort not to cry. This certainty alarmed him. He knew his wife's character, naturally hard, and hardened even more by forty years of bitterness. The death of her son had not wrung a single tear out of her.

He fixed a reproving look directly on her eyes. She bit her lips, dried her eyelids on her sleeve, and continued eating lunch.

'You have no consideration,' she said.

The colonel didn't speak.

'You're willful, stubborn, and inconsiderate,' she repeated. She crossed her knife and fork on the plate, but immediately rectified their positions superstitiously. 'An entire lifetime eating dirt just so that now it turns out that I deserve less consideration than a rooster.'

'That's different,' the colonel said.

'It's the same thing,' the woman replied. 'You ought to realize that I'm dying; this thing I have is not a sickness but a slow death.'

The colonel didn't speak until he finished eating his lunch.

'If the doctor guarantees me that by selling the rooster you'll get rid of your asthma, I'll sell him immediately,' he said. 'But if not, not.'

That afternoon he took the rooster to the pit. On his return he found his wife on the verge of an attack. She was walking up and down the hall, her hair down her back, her arms spread wide apart, trying to catch her breath above the whistling in her lungs. She was there until early evening. Then she went to bed without speaking to her husband.

She mouthed prayers until a little after curfew. Then the colonel got ready to put out the lamp. But she objected.

'I don't want to die in the dark,' she said.

The colonel left the lamp on the floor. He began to feel exhausted. He wished he could forget everything, sleep forty-four days in one stretch, and wake up on January 20th at three in the afternoon, in the pit, and at the exact moment to let the rooster loose. But he felt himself threatened by the sleeplessness of his wife.

'It's the same story as always,' she began a moment later. 'We put up with hunger so others can eat. It's been the same story for forty years.'

The colonel kept silent until his wife paused to ask him if he was awake. He answered that he was. The woman continued in a smooth, fluent, implacable tone.

'Everybody will win with the rooster except us. We're the only ones who don't have a cent to bet.'

'The owner of the rooster is entitled to twenty per cent.'

'You were also entitled to get a position when they made you break your back for them in the elections,' the woman replied. 'You were also entitled to the veteran's pension after risking your neck in the civil war. Now everybody has his future assured and you're dying of hunger, completely alone.'

'I'm not alone,' the colonel said.

He tried to explain, but sleep overtook him. She kept talking dully until she realized that her husband was sleeping. Then she got out of the mosquito net and walked up and down the living room in the darkness. There she continued talking. The colonel called her at dawn.

She appeared at the door, ghostlike, illuminated from below by the lamp which was almost out. She put it out before getting into the mosquito netting. But she kept talking.

'We're going to do one thing,' the colonel interrupted her.

'The only thing we can do is sell the rooster,' said the woman.

'We can also sell the clock.'

'They won't buy it.'

'Tomorrow I'll try to see if Alvaro will give me the forty pesos.'

'He won't give them to you.'

'Then we'll sell the picture.'

When the woman spoke again, she was outside the mosquito net again. The colonel smelled her breath impregnated with medicinal herbs.

'They won't buy it,' she said.

'We'll see,' the colonel said gently, without a trace of change in his voice. 'Now, go to sleep. If we can't sell anything tomorrow, we'll think of something else.'

68

He tried to keep his eyes open but sleep broke his resolve. He fell to the bottom of a substance without time and without space, where the words of his wife had a different significance. But a moment later he felt himself being shaken by the shoulder.

'Answer me.'

The colonel didn't know if he had heard those words before or after he had slept. Dawn was breaking. The window stood out in Sunday's green clarity. He thought he had a fever. His eyes burned and he had to make a great effort to clear his head.

'What will we do if we can't sell anything?' the woman repeated.

'By then it will be January 20th,' the colonel said, completely awake. 'They'll pay the twenty per cent that very afternoon.'

'If the rooster wins,' the woman said. 'But if he loses. It hasn't occurred to you that the rooster might lose.'

'He's one rooster that can't lose.'

'But suppose he loses.'

'There are still forty-four days left to begin to think about that,' the colonel said.

The woman lost her patience.

'And meanwhile what do we eat?' she asked, and seized the colonel by the collar of his flannel night shirt. She shook him hard.

It had taken the colonel seventy-five years – the seventy-five years of his life, minute by minute – to reach this moment. He felt pure, explicit, invincible at the moment when he replied:

'Shit.'

GABRIEL GARCÍA MÁRQUEZ

MEMORIES OF MY MELANCHOLY WHORES

'A Velvety pleasure to read. Márquez has composed, with his usual sensual gravity and Olympian humour, a love letter to the dying light.' John Updike

'The year I turned ninety, I wanted to give myself a gift of a night of wild love with an adolescent virgin...'

He has never married, never loved and never gone to bed with a woman he didn't pay. But on finding a young girl naked and asleep on the brothel owner's bed, a passion is ignited in his heart – and he feels, for the first time, the urgent pangs of love.

Each night, exhausted by her factory work, 'Delgadina' sleeps peacefully whilst he watches her quietly. During these solitary early hours, his love for her deepens and he finds himself reflecting on his newly found passion and the loveless life he has led. By day, his columns in the local newspaper are read avidly by those who recognise in his outpourings the enlivening and transformative power of love.

'Márquez describes this amorous, sometimes disturbing journey with the grace and vigour of a master storyteller' *Daily Mail*

'There is not one stale sentence, redundant word or unfinished thought' *The Times*

GABRIEL GARCÍA MÁRQUEZ

IN EVIL HOUR

'A masterly book' *Guardian*

'César Montero was dreaming about elephants. He'd seen them at the movies on Sunday ...'

Only moments later, César is led away by police as they clear the crowds away from the man he has just killed.

But César is not the only man to be riled by the rumours being spread in his Colombian hometown – under the cover of darkness, someone creeps through the streets sticking malicious posters to walls and doors. Each night the respectable townsfolk retire to their beds fearful that they will be the subject of the following morning's lampoons.

As paranoia seeps through the town and the delicate veil of tranquility begins to slip, can the perpetrator be uncovered before accusation and violence leave the inhabitants' sanity in tatters?

'*In Evil Hour* was the book which was to inspire my own career as a novelist. I owe my writing voice to that one book!' Jim Crace

'Belongs to the very best of Márquez's work ... Should on no account be missed' *Financial Times*

'A splendid achievement' *The Times*

GABRIEL GARCÍA MÁRQUEZ

INNOCENT ERÉNDIRA AND OTHER STORIES

'These stories abound with love affairs, ruined beauty, and magical women. It is the essence of Marquez' *Guardian*

'Eréndira was bathing her grandmother when the wind of misfortune began to blow …'

Whilst her grotesque and demanding grandmother retires to bed, Eréndira still has floors to wash, sheets to iron, and a peacock to feed. The never-ending chores leave the young girl so exhausted that she collapses into bed with the candle still glowing on a nearby table – and is fast asleep when it topples over …

Eight hundred and seventy-two thousand, three hundred and fifteen pesos, her grandmother calculates, is the amount that Eréndira must repay her for the loss of the house. As she is dragged by her grandmother from town to town and hawked to soldiers, smugglers and traders, Eréndira feels herself dying. Can the love of a virgin save the young whore from her hell?

'It becomes more and more fun to read. It shows what "fabulous" really means' *Time Out*

'Marquez writes in this lyrical, magical language that no-one else can do' Salman Rushdie

'One of this century's most evocative writers' Anne Tyler

GABRIEL GARCÍA MÁRQUEZ

NEWS OF A KIDNAPPING

'A story only a writer of Márquez's stature could tell so brilliantly'
Mail on Sunday

'She looked over her should before getting into the car to be sure no one was following her ...'

Pablo Escobar: billionaire drugs baron; ruthless manipulator, brutal killer and *jefe* of the infamous Medellín cartel. A man whose importance in the international drug trade and renown for his charitable work among the poor brought him influence and power in his home country of Colombia, and the unwanted attention of the American courts.

Terrified of the new Colombian President's determination to extradite him to America, Escobar found the best bargaining tools he could find: hostages.

In the winter of 1990, ten relatives of Colombian politicians, mostly women, were abducted and held hostage as Escobar attempted to strong-arm the government into blocking his extradition. Two died, the rest survived, and from their harrowing stories Márquez retells, with vivid clarity, the terror and uncertainty of those dark and volatile months.

'Reads with an urgency which belongs to the finest fiction. I have never read anything which gave me a better sense of the way Colombia was in its worst times' *Daily Telegraph*

'A piece of remarkable investigative journalism made all the more brilliant by the author's talent for magical storytelling' *Financial Times*

'Compellingly readable' *Sunday Times*

GABRIEL GARCÍA MÁRQUEZ

THE STORY OF A SHIPWRECKED SAILOR

'A gripping tale of survival' *The Times*

'On February 22 we were told that we would be returning to Columbia …'

In 1955, eight crew members of *Caldas*, a Colombian destroyer, were swept overboard. Velasco alone survived, drifting on a raft for ten days without food or water. Márquez retells the survivor's amazing tale of endurance, from his loneliness and thirst to his determination to survive.

The Story of a Shipwrecked Sailor was Márquez's first major, and controversial, work, published in a Colombian newspaper, *El Espectador*, in 1955 and then in book form in 1970.

'The story of Velasco on his raft, his battle with sharks over a succulent fish, his hallucinations, his capture of a seagull which he was unable to eat, his subsequent droll rescue, has all the grip of archetypal myth. Reads like an epic' *Independent*

GABRIEL GARCÍA MÁRQUEZ

OF LOVE AND OTHER DEMONS

'Superb and intensely readable' *Time Out*

'*An ash-gray dog with a white blaze on its forehead burst onto the rough terrain of the market on the first Sunday of December ...*'

When a witch doctor appears on the doorstep of the Marquis de Casalduero prophesizing a plague of rabies in their Colombian seaport, he dismisses her claims – until, that is, he hears that his young daughter, Sierva María, was one of four people bitten by a rabid dog, and the only one to survive.

Sierva María appears completely unscathed – but as rumours of the plague spread, the Marquis and his wife wonder at her continuing good health. In a town consumed by superstition, it's not long before they, and everyone else, put her survival down to a demonic possession and begin to see her supernatural powers as the cause of the town's woes. Only the young priest charged with exorcising the evil spirit recognizes the girl's sanity, but can he convince the town that it's not her that needs healing?

'Brilliantly moving. A tour de force' A.S. Byatt

'A compassionate, witty and unforgettable masterpiece' *Daily Telegraph*

'At once nostalgic and satiric, a resplendent fable' *Sunday Times*

He just wanted a decent book to read ...

Not too much to ask, is it? It was in 1935 when Allen Lane, Managing Director of Bodley Head Publishers, stood on a platform at Exeter railway station looking for something good to read on his journey back to London. His choice was limited to popular magazines and poor-quality paperbacks – the same choice faced every day by the vast majority of readers, few of whom could afford hardbacks. Lane's disappointment and subsequent anger at the range of books generally available led him to found a company – and change the world.

'We believed in the existence in this country of a vast reading public for intelligent books at a low price, and staked everything on it'
Sir Allen Lane, 1902–1970, founder of Penguin Books

The quality paperback had arrived – and not just in bookshops. Lane was adamant that his Penguins should appear in chain stores and tobacconists, and should cost no more than a packet of cigarettes.

Reading habits (and cigarette prices) have changed since 1935, but Penguin still believes in publishing the best books for everybody to enjoy. We still believe that good design costs no more than bad design, and we still believe that quality books published passionately and responsibly make the world a better place.

So wherever you see the little bird – whether it's on a piece of prize-winning literary fiction or a celebrity autobiography, political tour de force or historical masterpiece, a serial-killer thriller, reference book, world classic or a piece of pure escapism – you can bet that it represents the very best that the genre has to offer.

Whatever you like to read – trust Penguin.